How Water Shapes the Land

Written by Marilyn Woolley
Series Consultant: Linda Hoyt

WorldWise™
Content-based Learning

Contents

Introduction

Watch a rainstorm through your window. The falling rain flows over the ground and rocks. Look at how the little streams of water merge into bigger ones as rainwater moves downhill.

Much further away, where you cannot see, this water might be part of a large torrent or a fast-flowing river. As this water moves, it shapes the earth.

What you cannot see is how this rainwater is shaping the land we live in.

What happens when it rains?

All rainwater runs downhill. As it falls on the ground and runs downhill, it is called run-off. It runs into rivers and streams. Rivers are the main force in changing the shape of the land.

Where does rainfall come from?

Rain comes from clouds in the sky. But how did it get there?

The sun's heat evaporates water in oceans, rivers, lakes and plants turning it into **water vapour** in the air. The water vapour rises high into the sky and forms clouds. As more and more moisture builds up in the clouds, it starts to fall as rain, snow or ice.

This falling rain, snow or ice makes up all the freshwater on our planet. It is an essential part of our lives and the lives of all other living things.

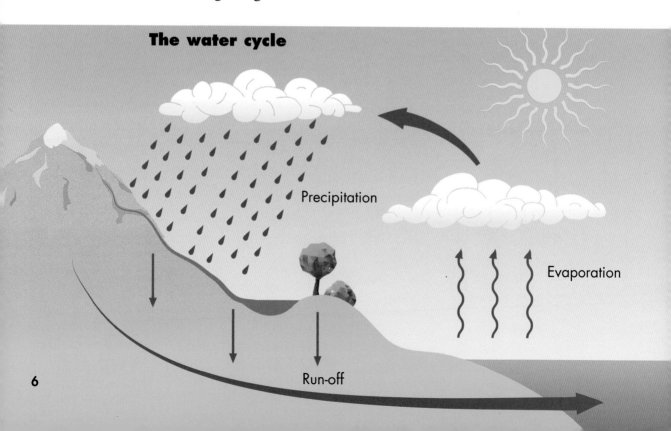

The water cycle

Precipitation

Evaporation

Run-off

Where does a river begin?

Rivers usually start high up in mountains, where there is much more rainfall than on flatter, lower plains. As moist **air currents** rise from the ocean to the land, they can meet the side of a mountain and bounce upwards. The air becomes cooler, clouds form, and then rain falls. This rainwater runs downhill. In some high places, the cold air forms snow, which is a solid form of rainwater. As some of this snow melts, it flows downhill. Melting **glacial** ice also adds to the **volume** of water flowing downhill. All this moving freshwater eventually forms a river.

A wide, deep canyon
In the state of Arizona, in the United States, the Colorado River runs through a deep trench for 1,600 kilometres. The deepest gorge made by the Colorado River is the Grand Canyon, at a maximum of more than 1.6 kilometres deep and 29 kilometres wide. The trip from top to bottom of this canyon and back again is a two-day journey on foot or by mule.

The river moves

In higher places where the land is steep, water in the river moves quickly and forcefully. It carves gullies in rocks. As the force of the water continues over time, the gullies become deeper. This is how gorges, deep V-shaped valleys and canyons are formed.

When water flows quickly over tall cliffs and rocks, it wears away the softer rock under the top layer. The water flows over the top of the cliff and falls over the edge. The fast-flowing water tears off boulders, bits of rocks and soil, and carries these along with it. As it does so, it widens the walls of the gorge, valley or the canyon.

How a waterfall forms

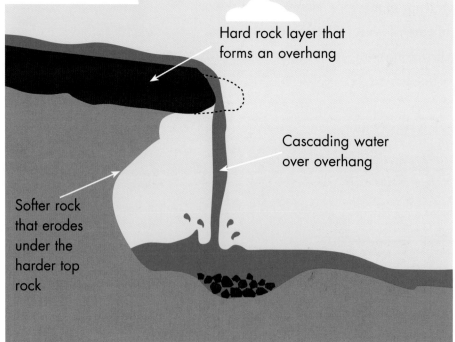

Hard rock layer that forms an overhang

Cascading water over overhang

Softer rock that erodes under the harder top rock

Did you know?

The flow-rate force is measured by the volume of water in a waterfall and how fast this amount of water is rushing down vertically by the pull of gravity.

American Falls

Horseshoe Falls

Bridal Veil Falls

Huge waterfalls

At the border of Canada and the United States, the Niagara River flows and connects two of the Great Lakes: Lake Erie and Lake Ontario. Over time, this river has carved a pathway through and over the Niagara Escarpment, a tall rocky ridge.

There are three separate waterfalls – American Falls, Horseshoe Falls and Bridal Veil Falls. Ninety per cent of this water goes over Horseshoe Falls. About 136 million litres of water flow over this waterfall every minute – that's enough water to fill 4,000 fire engines.

Although a **hydro-electricity** power station was constructed to interrupt its flow, Horseshoe Falls still has the highest flow rate of any waterfall in the world.

Find out more

Where is the world's highest waterfall? How did these falls get their name?

9

The river widens

As the river flows downhill from steeper parts of the land, it brings mud and rocks along with it. This collection of mud and rocks is called sediment. Lower down, the slope of the land is gentle and the river flattens out.

Several streams join up with the river so the amount or volume of water in it builds up. This buildup forces the water out sideways. The river carves out more of the soil on its banks as well as underneath it, and the amount of sediment increases.

The water weaves around this sediment, and the river forms bends or curves and sometimes splits into two narrower sections. The river deposits some of the water and some of the sediment along its banks. This action forms a flat area called a floodplain or a swamp. After heavy rain, the river floods over its banks into these areas.

The Rapa River in Sweden

A river floods the forest along its banks

Okefenokee Swamp in Georgia, USA

Where the river meets the sea

The river continues moving slowly, making a very flat valley until it reaches sea level. This is the lowest point of the land and is at the edge of the sea. Many rivers follow this route. They dump all of their sediment into a fan-shaped pattern that is broken up by small streams or **tributaries**.

When this happens, the soil that is deposited forms a delta. This soil contains many nutrients from the river water, so it is fertile and people grow many crops. Although river deltas are **fertile** places, they can be dangerous for people to live there. Deltas are likely to flood, if the river has built up a lot of water as it moves.

The delta where Clutha River enters a lake, New Zealand

A river winding into the ocean

The Okavango Delta in Botswana

Find out more

Where is the world's largest delta and how much area does it cover?

13

What happens when rainwater seeps under the ground?

Did you know that there is a hundred times more water under the earth's surface than in all the rivers and lakes combined? Water under the ground is called groundwater. Much of the rock and soil underground is permanently saturated by groundwater. How does this groundwater get there?

When it rains and the water runs downhill, most of it seeps into the ground or trickles through cracks in rocks.

This rainwater forms large underground pools called reservoirs or makes underground rivers. Underground water builds up over time, and some of it may be forced up to the surface of the land. It seeps up through the soil or through cracks in the rocks. When it rises above the surface of the land, it is called a cold or hot spring.

Cold-water springs in the United States are found in the Thousand Springs area along the Snake River in Idaho.

Cold spring water can filter up through the soil or seep from cracks in underground rock or rock structures as it moves downstream.

In some places, groundwater comes into contact with hot rocks near volcanoes. The water heats up very quickly, building up pressure and steam, before rising as a hot spring.

How a geyser is formed

If the temperature of the underground water becomes extremely hot, the pressure forces huge jets of the water and steam to shoot up high into the air. This is called a geyser. The water in a geyser can be almost three times as hot as water boiling in a kettle.

How caves are formed

In other places, underground streams and rivers carve away limestone rocks to form caves. Limestone rock is softer than other rocks and soaks up water like a firm sponge. Chemicals in the water dissolve and erode the rock. Often the water forms long passages and tunnels leading to and from the carved-out cave.

Pohutu Geyser, New Zealand

In Wyoming, the Grand Prismatic Springs make up the largest hot springs in the United States, and they are one of the three largest hot springs on the planet. The hole is 90 metres in diameter and the water is 70 degrees Celsius.

Mammoth Cave in Kentucky, USA, is the world's largest system of caves. Native Americans are known to have explored and lived in these caves for thousands of years. Mammoth Cave was established as a national park in 1941 and is popular with visitors. In 2016, half a million people visited these caves.

Chapter 2

How frozen rainwater changes the land

Glaciers

Glaciers are like frozen rivers of ice. They begin in high mountainous and polar areas where there is permanent snow cover. Over time, masses of snow build up and form a heavy sheet of ice. When this ice sheet builds up to a thickness of about 100 feet, it begins to slide downhill as a glacier – it advances.

As glaciers slide downhill, they pick up rocks. Under the moving glacier these rocks are dragged against the surface of the land. They smooth out the land and create wide valleys.

About 280 million years ago, glaciers formed across about one third of the Earth's surface. Glaciers have shaped many of the Earth's landforms.

Within the last two million years, there have been glaciers in the South Island of New Zealand. Two of New Zealand's most famous glaciers are Franz Joseph Glacier and Fox Glacier.

Once reaching the sea, these glaciers now end just 300 metres above sea level in forested valleys. Warmer weather caused them to melt and as they retreated about 14, 000 years ago, they carved out depressions in the valleys that became lakes such as Lake Mapourika and Lake Matheson. They deposited huge boulders that formed **moraines**.

Fox Glacier in
New Zealand

Find out more

What proportion of land on Earth today do glaciers cover?

Milford Sound

Milford Sound, on the west coast of the South Island of New Zealand, is an interesting landform with a range of natural features that have been carved out by glacial ice. It is a fjord, a large narrow crevice, formed by the erosion of ancient glaciers as they moved from the mountains to the sea.

This moving glacial ice eroded rocks well below sea level, and formed a sheer narrow valley with high vertical cliffs on either side. Its walls plunge steeply beneath sea level to a depth of over 500 metres. The fjord is three kilometres wide and extends inland from the sea for 16 kilometres.

Milford Sound waterfall

Cleddau River in Fiordland, New Zealand

How a moraine forms

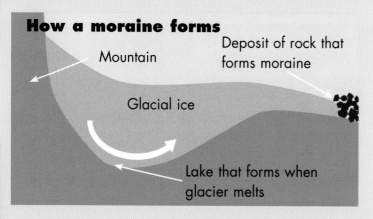

Mountain

Deposit of rock that forms moraine

Glacial ice

Lake that forms when glacier melts

The Cleddau River flows into the inland head of Milford Sound. It carries melted snow water from the Southern Alps down into Cleddau Valley. Along the path of this fast-flowing river is a chasm with a series of thundering waterfalls. The river formed the chasm as it eroded rock through a narrow valley. The water's powerful, swirling currents and the small rocks and gravel it carried with it have sculptured amazing natural patterns and shapes in the bedrock and surrounding rocks of the chasm.

Mountain peaks up to about 17,000 metres rise from the sea floor and surround the water in Milford Sound. Permanent waterfalls gush down from as high as 1,000 metres over the steep rock faces that line the fiord into Milford Sound waters. When it rains, the number of waterfalls multiply.

Milford Sound

Did you know?

A moving glacier can lift boulders the size of a house and carry them down to new places. The moraine deposited by the former glacier at the mouth of Milford Sound acts as a rocky barrier preventing large ocean waves coming into the fjord.

Mitre Peak rises 1,700 metres above fjord waters

A dwindling supply of freshwater

Freshwater is precious. It makes up only three per cent of all the water on Earth. It is an essential part of our lives and other living things. But some people have not always thought about freshwater as a limited resource, and they have not effectively managed the supply and use of freshwater. The needs of a growing global population, and increasingly prolonged droughts, have limited the amount of water available for all groups of people. About 780 million people around the globe still lack access to clean freshwater, and thousands die each day as a result.

How and why people are using more freshwater

People need water for drinking, washing and sanitation systems in their daily lives. They take this from rivers, lakes, wells or **reservoirs**. Over time, people's activities have interrupted the natural flow patterns of rivers and streams. They have pumped water out of rivers for irrigating their crops, and constructed canals and dams for these irrigation systems. Canals are also built to redirect water away from a river so that boats can transport people and goods to nearby houses, markets, businesses and factories.

Some large dams and reservoirs are built to hold back the flow of a river so that water can be piped to provide freshwater to cities and towns or to make **hydro-electricity** in power stations.

Think about ...

The construction of large dams, irrigation systems and hydro-electricity power stations on major rivers like the Colorado River in the United States and the Yellow River in China mean that these rivers no longer reach or flow into the sea.

21

The increasing number of people in the world has put pressure on freshwater river systems and lakes. People have built **levees** along riverbanks to try to prevent floods and this disturbs the water flow to other areas. Half of the world's wetlands have been drained when people have built houses and factories near them to have access to the water.

As well, higher temperatures and lower rainfall in some regions and countries mean increased demand for water.

Glaciers contain at least 70 per cent of the Earth's freshwater. If higher temperatures cause coastal glaciers to melt, the freshwater will flow into the sea and cause sea levels to rise and coastal towns will flood. Inland mountain glaciers will retreat during times of warmer temperatures, eventually reducing the volume of water that flows into rivers and supports large groups of people.

Find out more

Changing climate patterns are now leading to more droughts in places like Australia. What other places are experiencing prolonged droughts and what are the consequences?

Chapter 4

Freshwater management plans

Water-wise national and state plans

Many governments are establishing water management plans. These involve passing laws and regulations, and introducing new technologies to **harvest** rainwater, develop sustainable water practices and conserve the earth's precious freshwater resources. To help people cope with severe drought conditions, **hydrologists** build dams to store rainwater or install wells to bring water up from underground **reservoirs**.

Some national and state governments have added to the supply of freshwater by building large coastal **desalination plants** that convert saltwater to freshwater and pipe it to houses.

They are also building large water-recycling plants that clean wastewater and make it consumable to add to the supply from reservoirs and dams.

Some plans put restrictions on the amount of water that each farmer can take from a river and use for irrigating crops, and the amount of water that can be used for parks, golf courses and sports grounds.

A water-recycling plant

Flood-prevention plans

Other water management plans are designed to cope with too much rainfall.

When inland mountain glaciers melt, the freshwater flows into rivers, causing the flow of the river to become more powerful and surge forward. This floods lower areas of the land. At other times, huge downfalls of rain cause rivers to burst their banks, and water rushes over the surrounding land.

Think about ...

More than one billion people in Asia depend on rivers fed by Himalayan mountain glaciers for their food and livelihoods. They also get their electricity from river-fed hydro-electricity plants. Think about what will happen if these glaciers melt.

Warning devices

Hydrologists estimate the size of floods with GPS systems to establish the position of and the height of the river. They draw a cross-section of the river at particular points to help calculate flood levels. Engineers then design bridges or **weirs** for people to pass over the river safely when it is flooded. Stormwater drains take excess water away into rivers or the sea.

A hydrologist measures the flow of the stream.

A bridge over a flooded river

Floodwater flows into a drain.

Local city plans

In many cities around the world, rooftops and footpaths have hard surfaces so that rainwater cannot sink into them. Downpipes and stormwater drains take water away underground through pipes to flow into rivers. Several city councils in the United States are now using these drains as planting boxes to capture the rainwater in narrow lanes. Stainless-steel grates are placed under downpipes to filter out litter. The rainwater falls through these grates into the drains that have become garden beds planted with star jasmine and other climbing plants.

These city councils have also installed tree pits on footpaths close to the street kerbs above the stormwater drains. Each pit has a drainage pipe connected to the stormwater drain. A small tree is planted in a hole, and then a grate is placed around the trunk. The rainwater going into the pit saves having to provide extra water for the trees. These plants, in turn, help cool the city in hot weather and improve air quality. They also give off water through evaporation to create clouds and rain in the atmosphere.

Find out more

Find out about other cities or towns that have developed green alleys or tree pits on their footpaths.

Individual water-conservation plans

People now are thinking of new ways to conserve freshwater in their homes and gardens. They:

- use rainwater tanks to collect rain from rooftops to supply their own needs

- use less water to wash cars or hose gutters

- install showerheads that reduce the flow of freshwater

- use recycled wastewater for washing clothes, flushing toilets or watering their gardens

- choose more water-wise plants for their gardens and put timers on sprinkler systems.

Conclusion

Freshwater is on a constant journey in rivers as it moves from higher places and down to lower levels. Along its journey, it changes the shape of existing landforms and creates new ones. Many of the dramatic landforms shaped by water have become national tourist monuments. But freshwater is now considered a precious natural resource on our planet because the amount available for the increasing worldwide population is dwindling. Human activities in agriculture, industry and everyday life have interrupted the flow of rivers and reduced the amount of freshwater available. Governments and other groups of people are now seeking to find solutions to these problems while also working to conserve more freshwater to ensure the survival of living things.

Glossary

air currents the continuous movement of air in particular directions

delta the fan-shaped piece of land made by deposits of soil, found where a river runs into a lake or a sea

desalination plants factories where salt from seawater is removed to make the water suitable for people to use for things such as drinking and watering crops

fertile producing large amounts of healthy crops

glacial relating to glaciers, which are large, frozen, moving rivers of ice

harvest to gather or collect

hydrologists scientists who study where water is found on Earth, how it moves and its quality

hydro-electricity energy that is made using the power of moving water

levees barriers built to stop the overflow of water onto land

moraines mounds of earth, rocks and stones left behind by glaciers

reservoirs places where water is stored

tributaries smaller rivers or streams that flow into larger streams, rivers or lakes

volume the amount of space that is taken up by something, such as water in a river

water vapour water in a gas form that spreads out in the air

weirs dams built in a river to raise the level of the water or the direction the water flows in

Index